To all the people I loved before loving me

Janell Jay Roberts

you are me
oh you are me

and all the people

i loved before loving me

About me

Like many people, I grew up with little to nothing and writing became my way of feeling like something. Writing saves me when I feel like I'm sinking. It has taught me throughout my young life, to take the pieces of myself that scare me the most, and turn them into something beautiful.

I learned to turn the sadness into my *victories,* the homelessness into my stability, and my fear of God into my spirituality.

This poetry book is insanity, it's madness and yet beauty. These are my thoughts when I'm staring into space. It's the fake smiles, it's the *"I'm okay"* when I'm really not okay. It's the conversations with my therapists. And it's me, the hot-mess me.

Throughout this book, you will find that *most* poems have no punctuation, no capital letters, and many sentence fragments. I find the most compelling stories to be those of no break, no punctuation. Because It represents vulnerability, the smallness, and the mindfulness.

The pain of our trauma is universal, it will always be. The pain will always be there, but joy lives there too. It can, if you allow it. This is my first book, my first publication, my first child.

This is for the girl who lost her mom, to the man who's afraid to cry, to the *first generation college graduate* who is having a difficult time navigating the many facades of being a first gen. I write for you and only you.

It's to the abusive family dynamics we are trying to free ourselves from, and it's to the confusing and yet beautiful dynamic that comes with *finding you.*

So, I hope that in reading this short little book, you will feel strongly compelled to find your own creative voice if you haven't already.

So, please reach out, write me, email me:**contact@toallthepeople.co** or whatever the hell works best for you. Thank you, for allowing me to show you the thoughts that are in my head.

-jay

SECTIONS

1.YOU

2. THEM & YOU

3. YOU & LOVE

SECTION ONE

YOU

I want *you* to know that this section is for *you.* Because
you are the poems I write. *You* are the survivor, *you* are
the broken homes we fled from, *you* are the woman in
the mirror but most of all *you* are me and the many
women who look like we. *You* are the secrets we hide
behind locked doors, and the laughter that evades us in
the small moments we feel free.

This section is not beauty, it is not sunflowers and
rainbows, it is the darkness, the sadness, the laughter,
the self-loathe and everything else. This is to feeling
good, to feeling great, to feeling like shit the very next
day.

So, as *you* move through these pages, from section to
section, take this pain, and confront it, *you* don't have to
hide who you are here. I hope these pages make **you**
shout, I hope this section liberates *you*. But most of all I
hope it gives *you* a voice, so *you* can be the anchor for
people who feel the same way *you* do.

These are the poems to ourselves, these are our unsaid
words. This is *you* when no one is looking.

<u>sorry</u>

someone should have told you *sorry*
for all the times you lied awake at night crying to god
about how your mother made you feel so here i am saying
sorry for all the times you found yourself in the
sadness of someone elses eyes because your father
didnt tell you he loved you enough
im sorry that the good earth is both frightening and unfair
im sorry that the planet we
live in spews hate of what girls like you
black and brown in hue should look like
and im sorry for all the times
someone made you feel like
you werent enough

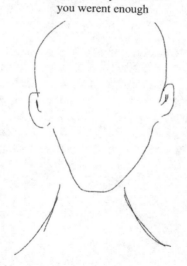

jay

alive and not well

i pushed myself into a box
just to make myself *feel small*

just to say *"i did it"*
just to shout *"i made it"*

only to realize that since the day
i was born
i had not been *living*

jay

a new way of thinking:

this is where the pain starts.
its your childhood - its your divorced
parents - or having no parents.
its losing a friend.

its spending time with a creepy family
member. its hiding being gay, its growing
up poor, black or islamic. we lose
ourselves to become someone else.

The pain is written in our history, forced
into our school system, pressed into us,
until we ~~those~~ are forced to
assimilate, forcing us to lose our
way.

(her-story)
The beginning of our history was tainted
by an uncertainty - and although this
journey hasn't been easy, you are a
woman of many facets, and being incomplete -

is not one of them!

people

and because youve *lacked*
self confidence since
you were a child
you have a hard time
figuring out what makes you
you
so you wear your *insecurities*
like school books
made for learning
and you refuse to be alone
because
you have a hard time
dealing with the unnerving
insecurities that kiss
your cheeks before bed
and
instead of dealing with the things you hate about
yourself
you continue to find a home in other
people
how sad it is
that you dont know what
your reflection looks like *in the mirror*
without a stranger staring back at you

you will outgrow your insecurities
you are not confined to disillusion

jay

YOU WILL SPEND YOUR WHOLE
LIFE SERVING OTHERS AND FIND
OUT AT THE END OF ALL OF IT,
THAT IT WAS ALL FOR
NOTHING.

NO ONE WILL EVER GIVE YOU
THAT SELF LOVE YOU ARE
LOOKING FOR.

LEARN TO LOVE THE SIDES
YOU THINK ARE UGLY, BY
EMPOWERING YOURSELF.

ULTIMATELY, YOU WILL FIND
THAT YOU HAVE THE CAPACITY
TO GIVE MORE TO YOURSELF
THAN ANYONE ELSE.

BE SELFISH FOR YOU,
EVERYONE ELSE IS DOING IT.

ive taken a lot

ive taken a lot of blows in life
broke a few bones

cried to god and
fought when i had to fight

i became a nuance
a ticking bomb and
i learned to distance myself from anyone
and everyone who got too close to me

i didnt want them to *feel* the explosion
feel the blows i had felt
feel the *madness* the *sadness* and
everything else

jay

a new way of thinking

you've been on your own for awhile
now. so alone, that you've lost touched
of who you are.

you often dont know how to
trust. you're constantly dealing with
the outside voices always ~~x~~ telling
you who you are

so practice this with me; close your
eyes and count to three. 1, 2, 3.

allow yourself to breathe. now repeat.
— there it is, that stillness you need.
And in this stillness you will find
that being imperfectly perfect is
a baptism of everything that
makes you gods, ~~father~~ favorite
masterpiece.

<u>you</u>

most of all
you deserve to know how important you are
because i know you dont hear it enough
and you need to know that there is so much love inside of you

s o   m u c h
that it scares people away and thats okay

youre the kind of person that deserves a godly love
for you love like *god*
and you should know that i see you even when you dont see yourself

because you are the sun in the early mornings
after a good nights rest when i wake up

jay

<u>*a place to rent*</u>

honestly

im afraid of being understood
understanding me both scares me and makes me afraid

all that i ask

is that you leave like the rest have
b e c a u s e

i am just a place to rent and never a place to stay

heres the truth
you will love you
more than anyone else ever will

you should learn to love you like you love others
like you love a lover or your mother

jay

tornado in the way

make sure you build walls up when i come around

make sure you hide underneath your beds
with all the people you love

make sure you build walls of steel
make sure you have a house made of cement
because when i come
i pray that you dont get in my way
because ive never had a home

and this is why i am this way

jay

<u>fireworks</u>

i thought that in the moments
i burn like fireworks

that i must fall in love with the warmth and
not the explosion the explosion being the
depression and the warmth being the *poetry*

i learned to inhale my familys chaos
instead of dealing with my own

i loved them too much
and myself too little

dont explode i tell myself
enjoy the warmth

jay

made to be this way

i was made to be this way
made to question everything
made to disrupt rooms
made to start *fights*
made to *scream* made to *shout*
made to make you feel like it was you and never me
made to blame you for every bad thing
thats ever happened to me

made to make you feel like you never deserved me
i was made in america the *land of the fucking free*

a place where there is no such thing for a *woman*
like me *loving* me for *me*

jay

Scream
as loud
as you want.

Shout when you
Need to - but do
~~Not~~ Not stay there.

too often we are
the only ones at
War with ourselves

in dreams

and you have the same dream every night
the one where youre trying to mold yourself
into what your mother and father couldnt be

those dreams that cripple you and make it hard
for you to rise and even *harder* to feel complete
i pray your children dont have those same dreams

the ones that seeps underneath your sheets
posing as *lovers* and false people

"who make you feel complete"

jay

<u>be careful with me</u>

be careful with what you say
my softness is a curse
i was taught to be this way

i will give you all of me until you cover
my entirety
and itll never be your fault
for i have a problem being this way

so be careful with me
im begging you

my mother

taught me to be this way

jay

and i grew afraid

i let a staleness hold my dreams
and it became a fear that crept up when i was alone in my bed
it became the *creepy* older family friend who watched me play

it became the *hot comb that burned my head*
it became school bullies
it became sleeping in cars with an empty belly

it became the *color of my skin*
it became a scream
a *scream* that i would carry into my twenties

it became a fear i could not escape and i grew afraid

jay

a new way of thinking:

the generational barrier that comes
with adulthood is inevitable. it festers
in your teens, and then implodes in your
twenties.

you carry it into your motherhood teaching your
daughter to be the same. But we can
overcome this by seeking therapy—
Holding ourselves tight and surrounding
ourselves around those who love our
entirety.

you will grow out of this, and you will
✻ bloom bright. But you are not alone, you
have never been alone, seek help, you deserve
It. Because we need you to be the light
for others — who feel the same way; but,
in ways they are unable to explain.

the hardest

and i know

that when i beat

d e p r e s s i o n

that i will understand
my power

that i will revolt against my
f e a r s

and that i will never
stifle in
t e r r o r

jay roberts

a new way of thinking.

Getting out of bed takes time, but
when you do it — there's a ~~subtle~~
subtle victory — you feel yourself
slowly but surely winning the battle
between yourself and the misery.

So keep silently. whispering:

"i can and i will, i
will and i fucking
can."

darkness

and that darkness swept over you again
wrapping its hands around your neck

the same darkness that you thought you freed yourself from

the same one that made it hard for you to get out of bed
you wrestled with it nearly losing your way

you wrangled with it as it grappled you
and you shouted
"no more darkness no more darkness"

as you screamed and wheezed to be free

"i will be free i will be free"

jay

talks with god

i dont need all the answers
i dont want them
i just need to know that youre here
that the loneliness i feel is only you bringing me closer to you
you dont have to teach me a lesson

i dont want to fight you
ill surrender to you
all you have to do is ask me to

because i need you when my days are blue
i need you when i cant leave my home or even go to school
i need you at work when im overworked and underpaid

i need you so badly
that when people see me
they see you

dear god
i am waiting for you

jay

<u>oh god</u>

and maybe ill scream to the stars
perhaps ill curse god
and ask her why she made my life so hard

and maybe shell answer
and perhaps she wont
but ill stretch my lungs out as far as theyll go

and ill shout to god that im tired of holding
on to things that dont make sense

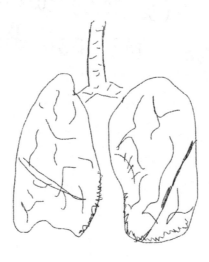

a new way of thinking:

Believe in something Bigger
than yourself. Whether it be
Allah, God, or Shivah, spirituality
is a gateway, it's the ultimate stepping
stone to loving you.

for me at least

God and meditation
helped me get through!

<u>broken people</u>

you liked broken things and shattered people

they were like puzzles of disguises
that helped you hide
everything you hated about yourself

jay

What if we invested all the time we invested into others into ourselves? How easy it would be- for us to identify which hands are drowning us, apart from those keeping us AFLOAT.

to the man i love

you were holding yourself in your arms
as if your body had no bones to keep you up
and you became confused and both afraid
of why you held yourself that way

"its okay to be both sad and afraid"
women arent the only ones
allowed to feel this way

oh man
i hope you free yourself from the
systematic oppression that made
"being sad" not okay

jay

dear oldest

oh quiet one
the apple of the eye
the one no one knows
especially when it comes to the *fear* you hold in *your eyes*

you hide the sadness that creeps up in your mind
and you make sure to *smile* so *everyone* thinks everything is *alright*

but dont hold it in release the voids
because

its wearing you thin
all of those voids

jay

<u>smile</u>

and when you smile

your smile never meets your eyes
because youre too busy *carrying*

peoples *sadness* until you
lose your mind

jay

ghosts

i hope that one day
you see that it wasn't you
it was me
and the ghosts that followed me

jay

myself

most of all

im just looking
for a safe place
to be myself

jay

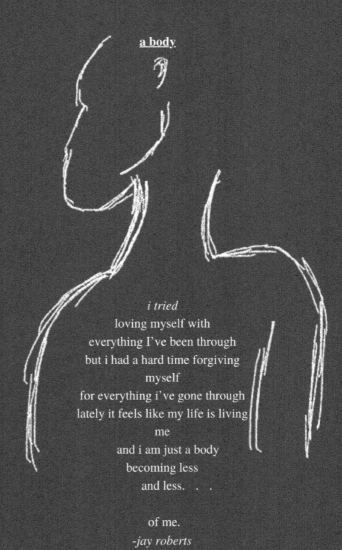

a body

i tried
loving myself with
everything I've been through
but i had a hard time forgiving
myself
for everything i've gone through
lately it feels like my life is living
me
and i am just a body
becoming less
and less. . .

of me.
-jay roberts

SECTION TWO

THEM & YOU

Them & you, is where our story starts. It's our history, it's the beginning, but yet, no ending. *Them & you*, are the words we wish we could say to the Narcissists we loved first before loving us. Whether it be our *socioeconomic status, the color of our skin, our struggle with religion,* or who we are forced to be for other people. *Them & you* is to the depression that we hide. It is the words left unsaid. It's to the sadness that almost conquered us and it's to the prayers that saved us.

Them & you is about the vulnerability you fear. it represents the way you smother yourself in other peoples worlds. It's the danger that starts you, it's the kickoff to the sadness and the landing of your insanity, it's the screams that never escape and it's the words we're afraid to say. this section is *for all the people who love too much and not themselves enough.*

Dramatic increase
in love/kindness

over protective
"Because they
love you"

after Abuse,
acts as if
nothing happened
will shower you
with "gifts, words
of Affirmation."

Narcissists
cycle of
abuse

Gains power
by forcing
you to "seek
Approval from them"

Will punish
you for having
an "opinion"
often through
Harm, control, &
verbal abuse

Controls what
you eat, who
you're with
but most of
all "How you
should _feel_"

the sadness

i was too busy folding myself over into all the people everyone
wanted me to be

i found out early on
that carrying everyone elses brokenness
made it hard for me to rise and even harder to feel complete

i wanted to run from my sadness like *my father* did
in hopes that maybe id find some peace

truth is

i am afraid to face myself
the broken me

the one who can no longer point the finger at others
as to why i havent worked on me
ive run out of people to blame

how sad it is knowing so much about yourself
and yet remaining the same

jay

wounds from you

there are moments
where certain wounds hurt more than others
these wounds keep me up at night
wounds i will never get over

im not upset with you
im just learning to love me
more than i loved you

but i will always love you
even when
*i walk on the opposite side
of the street to avoid you*

jay

narcissist

you wont find me smiling
youll never feel me in your *arms*

you wont hear my laughter or understand
the dust that made my *bones*

i may even tell you i love you even when *i dont*
and youll never notice the misery
because you never notice anything unless its about *you*

its hard for you to see things
when all you see is *you*

its hard loving a narcissist
when youre not even allowed to *love you*
you dont know how many times
ive prayed *for god to free me from you*
i want to learn to love me
without you and what you taught me too
because these fires in me
have a burning desire to get rid of the darkness

i call you

jay

<u>a new way of thinking:</u>

narcissists have the ability
to make you feel in-significant
and yet important at the same
time. you live for them and
only them, its almost as if you
were put on this earth to
only <u>love them.</u>

How scary is it, that it is often
the closest to us, mothers, fathers
and often time ~~lovers~~ lovers?

you can <u>not</u> allow these people
to make you feel small.
Read Books, talk to someone.
You deserve to be <u>free</u>, because
you were meant to be <u>free.</u>

.

im tired

i am tired
so very tired of being your doormat

on muddy days

as i watch you enter
the clean home

i built for you

jay

my words

i have a terrible past i know it
and sometimes my words feel like poison

yet
i am many things and yet nothing

truth is

im trying to understand how to exist with
all of the madness inside of me
because i know what its like to *behold and not to be held*

jay

THERE
IS NO WAY TO EXIST, NO WAY TO BE PRESENT,
WHEN WE ARE STUCK IN THE PAST.

OVERALL, THESE INSECURITIES,
PUSH YOU INTO ROLES WHERE YOU FEEL
NEEDED.

BUT BEING THAT PERSON FOR EVERYONE,
HAS ITS DOWNFALL. IT OFTEN ROBS YOU OF
YOUR ENERGY TO THE POINT WHERE YOU
OFTEN FEEL PARALYZED.

YOU HAVE THE BEST INTENTIONS
FOR OTHERS, SOMETIMES MORE THAN YOU DO
FOR YOURSELF.

BUT HERE'S THE TRUTH,

YOU WILL NEVER BE ABLE TO HELP
OTHERS, WHEN YOU HAVEN'T HELPED YOU.

<u>girls like me</u>

i thought i would snap in half
when you told me that your problems
were far worse than mine

girls like me had amounted to a victory
that finally made us equal to the men we see

you made me feel like i had bruised your heart like men did
like i was the plunders of your yells that your father left you with

and *i forgive you*
and all the things youve said to me
because now i know that it is impossible to speak to someone

who doesnt have

a pussy like me

jay

GOD
is
a WOMAN

<u>mother</u>

and i wondered why
my mother never heard me screaming for
help
in my writings
i guess my mother couldn't hear me over
her own inner mess
the sad poetry my father left her with.
she taught me that no one will love you like
you.
and this is why i never judge her for what
we've been through.
and
i know that the universe will support me,
for being the person my father couldn't be
for you.

-jay roberts

ill be there

and when you call for me
drunk on your own sadness
just shout my name to the stars
and ill be there
using *my soul t*o keep you warm
just as *i always* have long before god made me yours

all i ask is that you hold me in return
because sometimes it feels like my body
is crumbling underneath yours
and you must know that the drunkenness of your yells
are the things im running from

jay

enough

i knew that if i ever told you how you made me feel
that laughter would fill you

you were too damaged to understand
how hurtful your words were

i want to tell you that loving you is hard
i want to tell you that i am enough

i have always been enough

i am the diamond
you tried so hard to break
in the rough

jay

With time, i
am learning to
love myself, through
the storms i
often call tears.

<u>hurt</u>

you wanted to tell them how they hurt you

how you skinned your knees
so they wouldnt fall
you gave them all of you even when

you had a hard time feeling anything at all

jay

<u>temporary</u>

and *god if youre there*

you must know that
im tired of sleeping

a l o n e

with strangers in my arms

jay

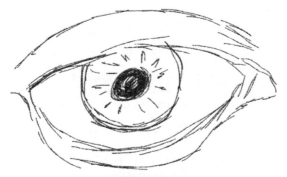

brown eyes

when you see these brown eyes what do you see
do you see the *poet*
do you see the *black woman*
the *poor woman*
my mother
or do you see me

because my brown eyes are an unnerving symbolism
of an endless wonder of who i was *forced to be*

and maybe one day
ill learn to smile without it being because
of you but instead

because of me

jay

nooses

i remember when you wrapped
your insecurities
around my neck

like nooses made for hanging

as you watched *the air*
that *pumped* my
lungs *leak away into yours*

as i cried in your ears

please

let me

breathe

jay

<u>yours</u>

i could tell that your exhaustion

steamed from all the people
you loved *first*

before loving you

jay

<u>hollow</u>

you rolled around in your sadness
as if they were *blankets of warmth*
as you cried in the realm of my chest
about ex lovers who crawled in your bed
as if you were *a place to rent* and never
a place to stay

you thought your sadness could drive
me away
and i tried to tell you that the
fault in your eyes were beautiful
even when you didnt understand

you were so hollow
that it made you mad

so i bought you a house so you could
see

whats it feels like
to *have your own home*
instead of being a *6 month lease*
that ends

jay

even if it means

i remember in the moments
you cried about fearing the darkness
how i got down on my knees

and prayed to a god
i didnt believe to make you feel whole even if it meant
not *being with me*

i just want you to be free cant you see

from all the *bad things*
your family did to you

but most of all from
what its doing to *me*

jay

HOW TERRIFYING IT
IS

THAT YOU PLANT
YOUR TRAUMA IN
PEOPLE

AS IF THEY GREW IT
IN YOU

<u>*dad*</u>

dad i talk to you
all the time in my head

jay

<u>baby boy</u>

i tried to hold you
like your momma did
when the world told you
that boys like you couldnt cry

i told you i loved you over
and over again
even when you *feared your own manliness*

its okay to cry we all do it sometimes

i said to you with tears in my eyes

jay

a _New way_ of _thinking_:

Who's hurt us, has nothing to
do with where we are now.
The world gives you choices—
make them or dont.

Just dont blame anyone, because
you decided to carry the
pain, when _God_ tried carrying
it _For you_.

please stay

you tried to warn me before i lost my way
but you were too late
i had already molded myself
into what *little boys* and *little men* thought was okay

you tried to tell me how the moon saw me
but i wouldnt listen you *were too late*

and i watched you walk away
with *my heart* in your hands

and tears down my face

jay

im scared too

"lift your hands up and dont move"

thats what the color of my skin
can do to people who look like you
i scare you
and *you scare me too*
but i want you to understand
that i probably like the same music as you

and *maybe we were*
friends when we were kids
before the world taught us the color of our skin

i forgive you i do
but i need you to understand

that i am scared of you too

jay

<u>here i am</u>

"look at me" you said with love in
your eyes

*"i do not care where i am as long
as i am with you"* i whispered
locking your hand in mine

"thats the problem" i mumbled with
fear in my eyes

*"i get sad sometimes i want you with me
all the time"*

jay

<u>i see you</u>

"i see you" you said to me

i closed my eyes
because you made me nervous
when you used that tone with me

*"im not those people who hurt you
i need you to trust me"*
you pleaded so desperately

*"i want you to **want me**
not need"*

jay

IT HASN'T ALWAYS BEEN EASY FOR YOU.
THERE ARE MOMENTS
WHERE YOU TRULY BELIEVE SOMETHING IS
WRONG WITH YOU.

YOU OFTEN HAVE A DIFFICULT TIME
BELIEVING THAT SOMEONE CAN LOVE YOU,
FOR YOU.

YOU ARE A SENSITIVE
PERSON AND THAT SENSITIVITY, COMES WITH
A DEEP AWARENESS THAT ALLOWS YOU TO
FEEL HOW PEOPLE AROUND YOU ARE FEELING.
WHICH OFTEN LEADS YOU TEND TO EVERYONE
ELSE'S
FEELINGS BEFORE YOUR OWN.

TOO OFTEN YOU GET CONFUSED ON WHO YOU
SHOULD BE FOR YOU, AND FOR OTHER
PEOPLE. YOU HAVE TO STOP BLAMING THE
ABUSE, AND LEARN THAT
SOME PEOPLE JUST WANT TO LOVE YOU FOR
WHO YOU ARE, AS WELL AS WHAT YOU'VE
BEEN
THROUGH.

the sun and you

i carried all of your trauma
and all of your pain
as if i were the one who *planted it in you*

i held you with tired arms
rubbed your feet when your legs gave up
and prayed with you

but listen to me when i say to you
it is your fault for carrying all of that pain

your family put you through

and maybe once you do
you will understand why we need the sun

so you can understand
why *i love you*

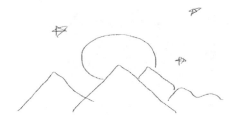

jay

stand with me

i *pray* you stand in solidarity
with me
with women who look like we
brown black and hue

i pray you stand with us
i pray you pray for us
but most of all i pray you use your *privilege* to
elevate us

i guess what im trying to explain to you
is that
we are tired
so very tired of doing all the work

while you stomp on our necks with your shoes

jay

<u>your homeboys</u>

i just wish you would
leave those people behind

those *"fuckboys"*
that make fun of you for
loving a woman like me

i just wish you would see
that even your *homeboys*
want a woman like me

jay

IT FEELS GOOD BEING
FREE

IT IS THE ONLY THING
NO MAN OR WOMAN CAN
TAKE FROM ME

I GUESS THATS JUST
THE WOMANISTS IN ME

the woman in me

"what are you afraid of" she asks

"i have to be strong"

"for who?" she demands

"for me and you cant you see
that we have to be strong
in order to break free
we cry behind closed doors
but not here
not we
we are women
yes we are women
and we must save the sadness
for when were alone in our rooms
underneath our sheets"

jay

SECTION THREE

YOU & LOVE

"You and love" *is your water, your hydration after emptying yourself out. It is your spirituality. It is us breaking free from the influences that hindered us.*

Most of all, this section is your breath of fresh air, so breathe this in, fill this up with your lungs and make these words your own. These are the words people like you and me have a hard time saying.

So please, mark the pages, scribble on them and I hope you learn to love you, more than you love them. This section is a reflection of how I see you.

Furthermore, I hope you learn to forgive yourself for all the times you felt like you weren't enough. My love, you are more than enough.

So cheers, to loving you.

<u>break free</u>

you're upset now
because i broke free from you
i found me and you lost you
i dismantled my insanity
stood tall
and begged god to help me get through

you tried robbing me,

stealing the consciousness
of my inner peace
but i'm strong
i broke through
i always do

and i pray
that you break free too.

-jay roberts

STRUGGLE,
CAN NEARLY MAKE YOU FEEL AS IF YOU ARE
BLOCKED FROM LOVING YOU. YOU FEEL AS IF, THERE
IS NO WAY TO EXPRESS YOURSELF.

SO YOU CRITICIZE YOURSELF MORE THAN ANYONE
ELSE. THERE IS ALMOST AN ENDLESS STRAIN OF
PAIN, THAT YOU HAVE YET TO RECOVER FROM.

IT CAN BE FROM YOUR CHILDHOOD, A PARENTAL
FIGURE, A BULLY, OR EVEN LOSING A CLOSE FAMILY
MEMBER. YOU OFTEN FEEL LIKE YOU NEVER HAVE
ALL OF THE ANSWERS – SO YOU JUST TELL PEOPLE
WHAT THEY WANT TO HEAR.

BUT LISTEN TO ME, YOU HAVEN'T DONE A SINGLE
THING WRONG. THE STRUGGLE THAT COMES WITH
LOVING WHO YOU ARE, IS THE WARRIOR YOU NEED!

TAKE A MOMENT, AND REALIZE THAT YOU ARE
EVOLVING INTO SOMETHING MORE, YOU ARE
LEARNING TO LET GO.

YOU ARE PUSHING YOURSELF TO BE MORE MATURE.
EVERYDAY IS A VICTORY AS YOU'RE LEARNING TO
SAVE YOURSELF FROM THE SADNESS, AND
DEPRESSION.

made to be great

we are made to be great made to start a fire
made to *drink* wine
made to *sing* a song
made to *cry*
laugh and maybe cry some more
made to fall in *love*
made to have *sex*
made to be straight *gay*
or be whomever we want

we are made to love and be loved
by a very special someone

so get rid of those people
who make you feel like its not okay

because it is okay to not always be okay
we must acknowledge this first so we can keep on carrying on
we are made to be more oh so much more
than all the bad things weve been through

for you are beautiful

and i am too make sure you find people

who sees you

for you

jay

<u>love you</u>

i found out that feeling beautiful doesn't come
from my lovers words but instead from the plunders
of my scars i hide underneath my clothes
from ex-lover's who used
my body as punching bags. i found out that feeling
beautiful doesn't come from
the constant comparison i do to girls
who look like me - but better

and now that i am found

i find
myself
in the *ache of my being*
learning to love myself with all
of the insanity

-*jay roberts*

<u>vowed</u>

and you *vowed* to yourself
that when you had a daughter
that she will know love
and love will know her

you vowed that your words
would kiss her ears before any mans did

and you vowed to hold her in ways
your mother never did

jay

beauty

im creating my own peace
as i learn to love every torn

and beautiful thing

that comes
with being me

jay

She may
be broken,
but she knows
how to build!

to sleep

i remember the first time i had *felt this way*
i was on my grandaddys farm

it wasnt a great farm
it didnt have horses or pigs
didnt have a big house
but it had cows and a tall oak tree

we were always at *someones house*
never *our own*

i remember always *waiting*
just being *patient*
until my momma could find somewhere for us to sleep

and now that im *23*
ive learned
that my home
is wherever god plants her feet

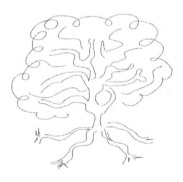

jay

a New Way of Thinking

No Matter where you Are,
No Matter where you Go —

The Earth is always around you.
The air is breathable, the
sky covers the entire world
and God is accessible. So
whenever you're lonely, sad
or simply confused —

Plant your feet,
Take A Moment
and find your
PEACE.

<u>dear me</u>

i wish you would understand
that i would throw myself into the ocean
even if i couldnt swim

i want you to know
that i will love you through the darkness

jay

<u>at birth</u>

it was like *us girls* were
pinned against each other since birth
like there was only room for one of us
like man was the only one who could love us

and

i wish i wouldve known what i know now
that we shouldve loved each other without the chaos

the chaos that came with *heteronormative*
decisions and not from us

jay

<u>walls</u>

and you make my walls fall down
youre my *sanctuary*
my *mausoleum*
my *prayers*
my sun and my stars

there are *no clouds* when im with you

because you are the *sun* that explodes
through my windows on rainy days
the days that are hardest to get out of bed

jay

forgive me

and i knew that if i were ever reborn
that id ask god to *forgive me*
for all the times

i saw you *sinking* as you made sure i *swam*

jay

Beloved

and i know im
not always the nicest
but please remember that
you are my one and
only love and that im
sorry for doing to you
all the things my
family did to me

dear thunder

you should know that i see you
even when your *yells*
sound like *thunder* across the night sky

you must know
that you are the backbone
that keeps things high

and that i will never fear
the sound of your cries

jay

<u>it got to me</u>

i tell myself over and over again that im okay
and that no pain lives in me

and now that ive accepted the truth
that comes with *being me*
i can freely say that there was a time

the *depression* got to me

jay

ITS EASY TO GIVE INTO OUR FEARS
WHEN LIFE CAN FEEL TIRESOME,
AND UNSATISFYING.

DEALING WITH DEPRESSION,
IS KNOWING YOU'RE DEPRESSED
AND FEELING AS IF YOU HAVE NO WAY OUT OF
IT.
OFTEN TIMES, WE TRY TO ESCAPE THIS
"REALITY" WHETHER IT BE WITH A
PERSON, OR A SUBSTANCE.

WORK
ON CALMING THESE VOICES, BY LEARNING TO
BE STILL WITH YOURSELF.
THIS
KIND OF COMPASSION IS WHAT YOU DESERVE.

TALK
TO SOMEONE, ANYONE, A STRANGER, A FRIEND
THERAPY HAS A WAY OF WORKING WONDERS.

BUT
FIRST, WE MUST ACCEPT THESE EMOTIONS,
ACCEPTANCE
IS THE FIRST STEP IN LEARNING HOW TO HEAL.

<u>my own peace</u>

im creating my own peace
im gonna *shine for me*

i want to feel the relief
that comes with loving me
im gonna be free for *me*
not for you
not for my daddy
but for me
for *fucking me*

jay

<u>healing</u>

lately
ive been turning to the light
letting the sun hit my cheeks

learning to love the parts of me
that i used to think werent so pretty

i feel me so deeply
i hold myself so tightly

jay

<u>fear fears me</u>

i use to be afaid
i had been afraid all of my life
i was afraid of my step fathers foot steps
afraid of the ass *whoopings* i would get

afraid to be afraid
afraid to breathe afraid to move
afraid to disagree *in fear* of what would
happen to me

it was when i *left home*
that i lost the fear that lived in me

fear has learned to fear me
because i am me

knowing who i am is
something fear can never take from me

jay

Your environment,
Healthy or toxic has
a way of defining your
Reality. The Body has

A way of picking up these
signs without your mind
acknowledging it. Centering
yourself and allowing yourself
to be present, will help you
become less in-tuned
with the outside world and
More of your own.

<u>20's</u>

the confusing time that comes in your *20's*
is teaching me to be less terrified
of the struggle
and more inspired with the journey

with time
i am learning
to find beauty
and everything

jay

APART OF LIFE'S JOURNEY, IS LEARNING TO
LOVE YOUR OWN SENSITIVITY. ITS ABOUT
OPENING YOUR PERSPECTIVE.
AND EMBODYING THE GOOD AND BAD TRAITS
THAT MAKE YOU WHO YOU
ARE.

THIS PROCESS MAY NOT ALWAYS BE EASY; AT
TIMES YOU WILL FEEL EXHAUSTED, BROKEN
AND TORN APART.

AND YOU
MAY FIND YOURSELF STRUGGLING TO
UNDERSTAND WHO YOU REALLY ARE. BUT
THROUGHOUT THIS PROCESS, YOU MUST
LEARN TO ACCEPT THE MANY DIFFERENT
FACADES AND FACES,
THAT COMES WITH BEING YOU.

WHETHER
YOU SEE IT OR NOT, YOU ARE LEARNING TO LOVE
YOURSELF WITHOUT ANY AGENDA.

<u>without</u>

im learning to be alone
without feeling lonely

alone but Not lonely

jay

never again

i spent most of my life living in silence
i learned to hold everything in
including the suffering

but

never again
will i ignore the warrior
that lives inside of me

jay

<u>*letting go*</u>

im letting go
of whats hurting my soul

jay

covid-19

i miss my home because i always leave and never get to stay
but im gonna stay home today
i wish i could every day
im gonna let the beautiful sun rays in
im gonna drink a lot of wine
read some good books meditate *pray to god*
smoke some weed and watch some tv

im gonna be safe in my home
im gonna be free
im learning that the body needs *balance*
that the body needs sleep

its okay to stay home
okay to be still
nows a time to put you first

nows the time to let the body heal

jay

the feeling

i hadnt felt *alive* until i saw myself *naked*
hadnt been *made love* to until *i was asked*
what i wanted in bed

hadnt climbed a mountain until i did
i hadnt swam in the ocean until
the sun was too hot on my *skin*

hadnt cried to god until i forgave myself
for all the abuse i allowed myself
to be in

jay

more

you are more
oh so much more than what they made you to be

you are the night light in my room
when im scared to go to sleep

you are the arms that wake me up
and hold me after bad dreams

you are more

oh so much more
than what this world told you
to be

jay

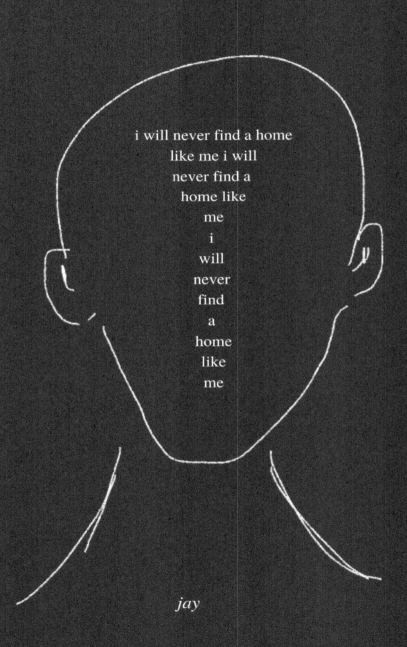

i will never find a home
like me i will
never find a
home like
me

i

will

never

find

a

home

like

me

jay

i am women

ive seen *women* climb mountains
start fires end wars and give life
ive seen *women* love back when life
was unkind
ive seen *women* give when they
havent be served

so what im trying to say to you
is that there is nothing you
cant do

being a *woman* means turning
your dissapointments into power
because theres a strength that moves
through you

so whenever you doubt yourself or simply feeling blue
remember that you have the power to build
even when there is no wood

jay

my own tongue

i stopped myself
biting my tongue
i caught my own negativity before it
could catch me
i killed it instantly
i stomped on my *"i cants"*
and swallowed my ***"i ams"***
i cleansed my thoughts out
and baptized myself in holy water

i targeted the flaws and prayed over them
i fasted for twenty something days

**what i am trying to say
to you
is that**

***i will kill the self hate
until it grows into self love***

i will love me more than
a***ll the people i loved before loving me***

jay

never going back

we will never go back
to sadness
to depression
exhaustion fatigue and weariness

lets promise *to never return nor accept*
the pre-corona extraction of being "happy"

lets raise a glass
have a toast

lets cheers to finally being able to "breathe"

so write the book
call your father
say your sorry
forgive yourself

how great is it
to be given the opportunity
to become one with yourself

jay

a poem
For
First Generation
College Graduates.

– Jay roberts

Dear First Generation College Graduate,

I know its hard for you, just as it is for many students who look like you.

But you should know that I see you.

That I hear the tears when you're alone in bed, and that I understand the sadness that crowds your mind when you're around friends who will never experience this "pain" you call your "own."

You are Brown, low-income and trying to navigate a world that was not created for someone who looks like you. But a world that wants to institutionalize you, hinder you, and even jail you.

But it gets better, surely you must know.

It's okay when your parents don't understand why you're having a harder time than the kids you go to school with.

It's okay to feel empty and confused. The pressure you feel is uncommon, and you must know that only the strong survive it.

You are more evolved than everyone around you, and your growth will pay off in due time.

But I know for certain that you're having a hard time believ ing that at the end of this everything will be all right.

Because, then you'll graduate, and you'll worry about work and making sure your family is financially okay. You'll feel like going to school was all for nothing - especially with the wunnerving loans you'll have to pay.

Dear First-Generation College Student,

I know you're killing yourself juggling three jobs, and five classes. I know your mental health is strained and that you're tired of feeling both, confused and afraid.

Your pain is normalized, and that is not okay. But you should know that just like you, Michelle Obama, Oprah and many others felt the same way.

I applaud you for being the first.

I praise you for being the leader when all odds are against you. You are the lamb that turns into a lion, and you are the sun that bursts through my windows on rainy days.

During the hard days, when you're unemployed, confused, and financially not okay, remember who you are and the bread you broke to make your life better for you and your family in order to pave the way.

For you are the moon, lighting up our darkest days. And you must know that I see you, even when you don't see yourself.

Dear First-Generation College Student, everything will be okay.

Sincerely,

A First-Generation College Graduate, trying to find her way

-jay roberts

thank you
for reading

Made in the USA
Las Vegas, NV
15 August 2023

76145778R00066